Career Quest

EXPLORING ENGINEERING CAREERS

ANDREW MORKES

TWENTY-FIRST CENTURY BOOKS / MINNEAPOLIS

Twenty-First Century Books™
An imprint of Lerner Publishing Group, Inc.
241 First Avenue North
Minneapolis, MN 55401 USA

For reading levels and more information, look up this title at www.lernerbooks.com.

Main body text set in Bembo Std Regular.
Typeface provided by Monotype Typography.

Library of Congress Cataloging-in-Publication Data

Names: Morkes, Andrew, author.
Title: Exploring engineering careers / Andrew Morkes.
Description: Minneapolis : Twenty-First Century Books, [2026] | Series: Career quest | Includes bibliographical references and index. | Audience: Ages 11–18 | Audience: Grades 7–9 | Summary: "From roller coasters to solar panels, engineers design all sorts of cool and useful structures. But how many kinds of engineers are there? And what does it take to become one? Discover the answers to these questions and more"—Provided by publisher.
Identifiers: LCCN 2024037250 (print) | LCCN 2024037251 (ebook) | ISBN 9798765644171 (lib. bdg.) | ISBN 9798765684870 (pbk.) | ISBN 9798765682739 (epub)
Subjects: LCSH: Engineering—Vocational guidance—Juvenile literature.
Classification: LCC TA157 .M6229 2026 (print) | LCC TA157 (ebook) | DDC 620.0023—dc23/eng/20241218

LC record available at https://lccn.loc.gov/2024037250
LC ebook record available at https://lccn.loc.gov/2024037251

Manufactured in the United States of America
1 – CG – 7/15/25

CONTENTS

INTRODUCTION

Many people want to enter a career in engineering because a variety of occupational paths are available, the work is intellectually demanding, no workday is the same, and the pay is above the national average for all careers. Plus, many people think engineering is fun! Engineers design roller coasters, spaceships, electric vehicles, and many other things. They also help solve world problems. For example, engineers have helped design structures such as solar panels that create renewable energy for people or buildings to use instead of pollution-causing fossil fuels.

This book covers everything you need to know about training for and being successful in a career as an engineer, engineering technician, or technologist. It details the history of the engineering industry, modern work environments and advancement opportunities, skills and projects to get you started early, how new technology is changing the field, and more.

CHAPTER ONE

All about Engineering

According to American engineer James Kip Finch, "The engineer has been, and is, a maker of history." Egyptian architect Imhotep, who designed and built the Step Pyramid at Saqqara, Egypt, around 2550 BCE, is the first engineer whose work and name are both known. The ancient Egyptians, Persians, Greeks, and Romans all designed and built many civil engineering marvels—such as the Colosseum in Rome, elaborate road systems, and the Lighthouse of Alexandria in Egypt—some of which still stand.

The origins of modern engineering can be traced to the seventeenth and eighteenth centuries when the laws of physics and mathematical principles began to be understood and developed. Then in the last 150 years, great leaps in medical science, building materials, computer technology, and manufacturing processes have expanded the types of engineers needed and the products and structures that they can create. Some noteworthy examples of the ingenuity of engineers and scientists include the invention of the electric motor (1886), the invention and first powered flight of a heavier-than-air aircraft (1903), the design and use of the first computer mouse (1964), and the design and first successful implantation of an artificial heart in a human (1982). Emerging technologies such as artificial intelligence (AI), quantum computing, advanced robotics, and the Internet of Things are expanding what modern engineers can do too.

Amazing Achievements in Engineering

The National Academy of Engineering is a nonprofit organization of experienced engineers who provide free advice to lawmakers regarding some of society's toughest challenges. It also selected the greatest engineering achievements of the twentieth century. These are the organization's top ten:

1. electrification
2. automobile
3. airplane
4. water supply and distribution
5. electronics
6. radio and television
7. agricultural mechanization
8. computers
9. telephone
10. air-conditioning and refrigeration

What Is Engineering?

Engineering principally involves the use of physics, mathematics, science, and technology to solve problems, design and create structures and products, and improve existing ones. There are many types of engineers.

Aerospace engineers use their knowledge of materials, flight mechanics, aerodynamics (the study of gases in motion), thermodynamics (the study of heat and other forms of energy), propulsion (the process of driving something forward), guidance and control systems, physics, and mathematics every day. They design, test, and help manufacture aircraft, helicopters, satellites, spacecraft, drones, and missiles. Specialties in the aerospace engineering field include aeronautical engineering (air flight within Earth's atmosphere), astronautical engineering (flight beyond Earth's atmosphere into outer space), and avionics (electronic systems such as those for communications and navigation). Aerospace engineers have played a major role in the field of space exploration since the 1950s, and as of 2024, these engineers are helping NASA and private space companies build spacecraft that will land people on the moon again. A history-making trip to Mars is also on the horizon. An emerging area of interest for aerospace engineers is hypersonic technology, which consists of aircraft, missiles, and other airborne objects that can fly at speeds of at least Mach 5, which is defined as a minimum speed of 3,836 miles per hour (6,174 kph). Much of this research focuses on developing offensive and defensive weapons for military use.

Biomedical engineers work at the forefront of science and technology. They use their expertise in mechanical, chemical, and electrical engineering; chemistry; mathematics; materials science; and human biology, anatomy, and physiology to design and develop methods to improve human health. They not only design devices such as pacemakers and orthopedic implants, but they also develop new diagnostic tools and medical equipment. As of the 2020s, research areas for biomedical engineers include stem cell engineering (to manipulate and control the behavior of stem cells to produce specific cell types or treat diseases) and the 3D printing of biological organs.

Chemical engineers create medications, food, gasoline and other fuels, biological products such as vaccines, paper, and many other products. They often study and know a lot about chemistry, biology, physics, and food science.

An aerospace engineer performs a repair on a jet engine. These engines are used to propel large aircraft at high speeds.

You can thank a *civil engineer* every time you switch on the lights, turn on the water faucet, and drive down a safe and well-designed highway. These multitalented engineering professionals design, build, and maintain the infrastructure that keeps society functioning. Infrastructure consists of communication, electrical, sewage, transportation, water, and related systems. Civil engineers also help design and build dams, airports, and many other structures. Common civil engineering specialties include construction, environmental, geospatial, geotechnical, structural, transportation, and water resource engineering. Some cutting-edge areas that they work in include self-repairing construction materials, green construction materials and practices, and renewable energy. Another area engineers might focus on is designing for resilience, which involves creating buildings that can better resist natural disasters such as earthquakes and extreme weather.

Computer engineers design, develop, troubleshoot, and maintain hardware and software. *Hardware engineers* focus on networks, routers, circuit boards, and other types of electronic hardware technology. *Software engineers* (who are sometimes known as software designers) develop system software or apps that allow users to do specific tasks on a computer, phone, or other electronic device. Apps can be used for everything from navigating in your vehicle to monitoring your health to tracking your finances. Many hardware and software engineers focus on developing computer games and gaming hardware that millions of people love. Their work increasingly includes integrating AI, augmented and virtual reality, and other technologies into the gaming experience.

Electrical engineers design, develop, test, and oversee the manufacture of power generation equipment, electrical systems of automobiles and aircraft, radar and navigation systems, robotics systems, computer hardware, communications systems, and other types of electrical equipment. If a product uses electricity, an electrical engineer has created or improved it. Major specialties of electrical engineering include control/automation, electronics, microelectronics, power system engineering, and signal processing engineering. New areas of work for electrical engineers in the 2020s include automated electric cars and next-generation smartphones.

Environmental engineers work to address the negative effects of pollution and industrial contamination on air, water, and soil quality. One of their biggest challenges is helping corporations, government agencies, and people respond to the negative effects of climate change, including increased droughts, flooding, wildfires, and other natural disasters and extreme weather.

Using genome engineering technologies, *genetic engineers* and *scientists* edit or remove genes to try to cure or prevent diseases and other medical conditions; develop new sources of bioenergy; and increase the shelf life, nutritional value, and flavor of fruits and vegetables.

Industrial engineers are skilled troubleshooters, brainstormers, problem-solvers, outside-the-box thinkers, and improvement specialists. They help companies save time and money, cut energy output, and reduce the amount of materials needed to produce a product. Examples of their work include automating a software development process, evaluating manufacturing processes to identify areas of waste, and assessing work functions of employees to improve staff productivity.

Manufacturing engineers design, develop, troubleshoot, and maintain the production processes and systems that are used to create everything from refrigerators, sports utility vehicles, and televisions to medications, packaged foods, and toys. *Advanced manufacturing engineers* work with nontraditional manufacturing techniques, such as nanotechnology, additive manufacturing (building an object layer by layer, such as in 3D printing), laser machining/welding, and computer numerical control machining. The tools they utilize include advanced data analytics, advanced robotics, artificial intelligence, big data (the study of large, complex data sets to reveal trends, patterns, and associations), digital design and prototyping, and virtual and augmented reality. They also use the Industrial Internet of Things, which incorporates smart sensors, actuators (devices that convert energy to power devices or machinery), and other devices—such as radio frequency identification tags—to improve industrial and manufacturing processes.

Materials engineers and *materials scientists* are experts on the materials that are used to build everything from integrated circuits to spacecraft. Examples of materials include polymers (natural and synthetic substances that are composed of very large molecules); metals and alloys; ceramics and glasses; electronic, magnetic, and optical materials; and composites. Engineers and scientists also work with emerging materials such as biomaterials (for example, artificial skin for burn victims); 3D printing materials; nanomaterials; and specialized sensors. Some work with smart materials—materials that are engineered to react in a controllable

Engineers use computer-aided design to create 2D designs, then print them using a 3D printer.

and reversible manner. Materials engineers and scientists often work in the aerospace, advanced manufacturing, construction, and semiconductor industries.

Mechanical engineering is one of the oldest engineering professions. *Mechanical engineers* design, build, and test robots, mechanical systems within buildings (such as ventilation, air conditioning, and fire protection), power plants, power-producing machines such as electric generators and internal combustion engines, and almost any other complex systems or equipment that are built. They also improve existing machinery, products, and manufacturing processes. There are many specialties in mechanical engineering, including acoustics, automation, biotechnology, nanotechnology production planning, and structural analysis. One emerging specialty is entertainment engineering. These engineers usually have backgrounds in mechanical, electrical, and materials engineering. They design, build, troubleshoot, and repair structures and systems that entertain people. Some of these include roller coasters; stage components for musical acts, theater performances, and sporting events such as the Super Bowl halftime shows; and water park rides. Mechanical engineers not only develop new types of cars, satellites, spacecraft, and roller coasters, but they are also using nanotechnology to engineer materials on the smallest of scales. "Nanotechnology is helping to considerably improve, even revolutionize, many technology and industry sectors: information technology, homeland security, medicine, transportation, energy, food safety, and environmental science, among many others," according to the National Technology Initiative.

Mechatronics engineers use knowledge of mechanics, electronics, communications systems, and computer software and hardware to create robots, control systems, smart devices, and electro-mechanical systems. Many work in the manufacturing, health-care, automotive, aerospace, and consumer electronics industries. Much of their work focuses on automation—creating robots and other technology that replace human labor.

Robotics engineers develop robots that are used in manufacturing, the armed forces, food preparation, and security. In the 2020s, these engineers are utilizing advanced artificial intelligence to create robots that can be trained to take actions and make choices on their own.

Additional Engineering Specialties

Those are some of the major engineering specialties. But engineering is a huge field, and engineers can find jobs in many different industries with many different purposes. While this book can't cover every specialty fully, here are some more engineering specialties to investigate:

- *Agricultural engineers* solve agricultural problems relating to areas such as power and machinery, soil and water conservation, and the processing of agricultural products.
- *Building automation engineers* create technology that controls lighting, heating, cooling, access control, and other systems without human intervention.
- *Forensic engineers* gather and study evidence at crime scenes, car accidents, plane crashes, and other events in order to present this information in a court of law.
- *Health and safety engineers* use their knowledge of industrial processes, mechanics, chemistry, and physics in the areas of workplace safety and product development.
- *Marine engineers* design and develop marine vessels, ship machinery, and power supply and propulsion systems.
- *Mining engineers* develop ways to extract coal, gold, and other minerals and metals from underground.
- *Nuclear engineers* oversee the safe development

and use of nuclear power, as well as the disposal of nuclear waste.

- *Ocean engineers* design, construct, and manage systems and marine vessels that are used in ocean environments (both below and above the surface).
- *Petroleum engineers* develop ways to extract oil and gas from underground.

An agricultural engineer inspects vegetables growing in a soilless greenhouse. Engineers in this field are researching ways to grow plants in new and sustainable ways.

Engineering Technicians and Technologists

Engineers would not be able to do their work without the assistance of engineering technicians and technologists. These workers handle tasks such as:

- cleaning, organizing, setting up, or otherwise preparing workplace tools, equipment, and materials
- collecting data and preparing it for review by engineers and scientists
- visiting worksites to gather data or to perform other tasks
- building prototypes from plans or sketches
- assembling, testing, and maintaining mechanical, electronic, or other types of components
- using computer-aided design software to create blueprints and schematic diagrams
- writing reports
- maintaining project files and records

Technicians and technologists also monitor quality control issues. "When it comes to quality management processes in engineering projects, the contributions of engineering technicians often go unnoticed," says MoldStud, a custom software development company. "While engineers play a crucial role in designing and planning, it is the diligent work of engineering technicians that ensures the implementation and maintenance of quality standards throughout the project lifecycle."

Engineering technicians and technologists allow engineers

Women in Engineering

In 2023 women comprised only 16.7 percent of engineering and architecture workers. This was much lower than the percentage of women in the workforce overall (46.9 percent). The percentage of women engineers is slightly higher in chemical engineering (21.6 percent) and industrial engineering (24.6 percent). But it is lower in hardware engineering (5.9 percent) and mechanical engineering (10.1 percent). But the overall percentage of women who are pursuing careers in engineering and architecture is on the rise. According to the Society of Women Engineers, just 9 percent of engineering and architecture workers were women in the 1990s.

Women have played an important role in the field throughout history. Some well-known women engineers include:

- Lillian Gilbreth (1878–1972): a pioneering industrial engineer and psychologist who conducted groundbreaking work in the fields of human factors engineering and workplace efficiency
- Edith Clarke (1883–1959): a trailblazing electrical engineer and inventor who invented the Clarke calculator, a graphical device that was capable of plotting graphs, solving equations, and performing other tasks in order to more quickly solve electrical engineering problems
- Mae Jemison (born 1956): a chemical engineer, physician, and astronaut (and the first African American woman to travel into space) who is, as of 2024, a science educator and owner of a technology consulting firm

- Frances H. Arnold (born 1956): a professor of chemical engineering, bioengineering, and biochemistry who, in 2018, became the fifth woman to be awarded the Nobel Prize in Chemistry for her work with the directed evolution of enzymes
- Ellen Ochoa (born 1958): an electrical engineer and astronaut who was the first Hispanic woman to travel into space (1993) and who served as the director of the Johnson Space Center between 2013 and 2018

Why are women underrepresented in engineering? Gender discrimination, sexual harassment, unequal pay, and few women role models are some of the factors that have limited the number of women who want to or are able to enter the field. Government agencies, professional associations, and companies that employ engineers have launched educational outreach programs, mentoring programs, and hiring initiatives to increase the number of women in the field. The following organizations provide great resources for aspiring women engineers, including membership, classes, publications, and networking groups:

- American Society for Engineering Education: Women in Engineering Division
- Association for Women in Science
- IEEE Women in Engineering
- National Society of Black Engineers: Women in Science & Engineering Special Interest Group
- Society of Women Engineers

to focus on more complex design or repair challenges. They typically specialize in a particular engineering specialty (such as civil or electrical engineering), although some are generalists.

At some employers, the job titles *technician* and *technologist* are interchangeable. At others, these titles represent distinct positions with specific educational requirements and job duties. At such an employer, a technologist is a worker who has earned a bachelor's degree in engineering and is assigned higher-level duties than a technician performs. Technologists may also supervise technicians and other technologists. A technician typically has an associate's degree in engineering technology or an engineering specialty.

Job Prospects

As of 2024, just over 2.5 million people are employed in engineering and architecture occupations in the United States. Here are the largest specialties:

- industrial engineers: 332,870 workers
- civil engineers: 327,950 workers
- electrical and electronics engineers: 281,840 workers
- mechanical engineers: 281,290 workers

Job growth is expected to be especially high in aerospace, agricultural, biomedical, chemical, electronics, environmental, hardware, industrial, materials, and mechanical engineering. Chapter five will cover predicted job growth in more depth.

CHAPTER TWO

Aspects of an Engineering Career

Engineers design and develop many products, structures, and technologies. But where do they work? How much are they paid? What skills make a successful engineer? And how do they advance in their careers?

Work Environments

It might seem like most engineers work in offices or design studios. But engineers also work in manufacturing plants, construction sites, water treatment plants, and laboratories. Some even work in outer space! Other engineers might work from home or other remote sites.

Salaries

Salaries for workers in engineering and architecture occupations are often well above the national median. The median annual wage for this group was $83,700 in May 2022, according to the US Department of Labor. This was higher than the median annual wage for all careers, $46,310. Additionally, the department lists these salary ranges for engineers and engineering technicians in various specialties. The top range is the highest reported salary, but engineers can receive higher earnings.

- aerospace engineers: $78,170 to $176,280
- agricultural engineers: $50,480 to $146,350
- civil engineering technologists and technicians: $37,430 to $85,740
- civil engineers: $61,040 to $138,690
- electrical and electronic engineering technologists and technicians: $43,930 to $101,480
- electrical engineers: $65,480 to $166,970
- industrial engineering technologists and technicians: $40,710 to $90,430
- industrial engineers: $62,730 to $134,990
- mechanical engineers: $61,990 to $151,260
- nuclear engineers: $79,440 to $169,580

Key Skills for Success

Engineering professionals must have a wide range of technical and soft skills to be effective on the job. Technical skills vary by position, but the ability to use computer-aided design software, computer modeling, and other engineering software to model, simulate, and analyze complex engineering systems is important in this field. Engineers must also stay up-to-date with emerging technologies, such as AI, nanotechnology, and augmented reality. Understanding these and other new technologies as they arise will help engineers to do their jobs more effectively. In some instances, new technologies can even be used to create new products or improve existing ones.

Soft skills are also important in the workplace because employers want staff who can work well with others and function effectively on the job. Some important soft skills for engineering professionals are:

- analytical and critical thinking abilities
- time-management and organizational skills
- patience and the ability to stay calm under pressure
- troubleshooting and problem-solving skills (including an understanding of how to use the engineering design process to solve problems)
- confidence and the ability to accept constructive criticism
- oral and written communication skills
- a design-thinking mindset
- being detail-oriented
- curiosity
- the ability to work both independently and as a member of a team
- ethics

Advancement Opportunities

Engineering professionals with extensive experience and who continue to expand their skills through continuing education can advance to higher-level positions. Continuing education consists of online and in-person classes that one takes throughout their career to improve their knowledge. Advancement usually comes in the form of a new job title, more demanding work duties, an increase in salary, and other perks.

Experienced technicians and technologists who have leadership ability can be named *lead technician* or *technologist*. They supervise the work of other technicians and technologists and interact more closely with engineers and scientists. Technicians who earn a bachelor's degree can advance to become technologists or engineers, and technologists can move up to become engineers.

Engineers who have strong leadership and managerial skills can become *lead engineers*, who manage less-experienced engineers, technicians, and technologists, as well as oversee projects. Lead engineers can move up to work as *engineering managers*, who create budgets and monitor spending, work closely with executives on current and future projects, and supervise a team of lead engineers. A *vice president of engineering* is the top engineering position at many employers. They work with company executives on long-term operational strategies and develop and improve hiring and training programs. They also conduct market and product research and oversee all lower-level engineering teams to ensure that product development deadlines are met within the expected budget.

Wind power is the fourth-largest source of electricity generation capacity in the United States.

Engineering professionals with strong managerial, business, and entrepreneurial skills may start their own engineering services firm. Or they might open a consulting firm that provides engineering expertise and services to companies, government agencies, or other customers.

Some engineering professionals decide to teach in apprenticeship programs or at community colleges, technical colleges, or universities. They teach everything from basic classes, such as introductions to engineering, to those at the advanced level, such as classes on advanced electron microscopy. Some professors continue to work in their specialty while teaching. Others work as full-time educators. Sometimes teaching opportunities are also available at middle schools and high schools.

But that's just the start of advancement options for engineers who want to remain in the field. Some use their engineering expertise in other fields. For example, Neil Armstrong, an astronaut who became the first person to walk on the moon on July 20, 1969, was first an aeronautical engineer. In fact, many astronauts have degrees in

In 2023 there were 38,370 college engineering educators in the United States.

engineering. Ellen Ochoa, the first Hispanic woman to travel to space, has degrees in physics and electrical engineering.

Other prominent professionals started as engineers too. Herbert Hoover, the thirty-first president of the United States, was an internationally renowned mining engineer before entering politics. Martin Heinrich, who has a bachelor of science in mechanical engineering, was elected as a US senator representing New Mexico in 2013 and still serves as of 2024. No matter where they start or what they specialize in, there are many opportunities for engineering professionals.

The Best Engineering Jobs

For many people, an appealing job provides a good work-life balance, low or manageable stress levels, a salary that is higher than the average earnings for workers in all careers, and strong employment prospects with lots of available jobs. Each year, US News & World Report assesses these criteria for hundreds of jobs and creates a list of the one hundred best careers in the United States. Here are its top engineering-related careers. The overall ranking out of one hundred for each career appears in parentheses after each entry.

- mechanical engineer (18)
- environmental engineer (34)
- biomedical engineer (60)
- civil engineer (84)
- cartographer (95)
- architect (99)

CHAPTER THREE

Starting Your Career in Engineering

Exploring Education and Careers in Engineering

It's never too early to start exploring the world of engineering. Doing so will help you determine if engineering is right for you and which specialty is the best fit. Or perhaps you'll decide to become a technician or technologist instead of an engineer. There are many hands-on and other exploratory activities that you can do to learn more about the field and obtain experience. These range from something as simple as watching a film about engineering to testing your engineering knowledge skills in a competition or attending a summer engineering camp.

Join or Use the Resources of Professional Associations

Professional associations exist to serve the needs of workers in a particular occupation (such as civil, industrial, or mining engineering) or industry (such as engineering or health care). They may also represent members of specific genders or racial or ethnic groups. These organizations provide a wealth of resources, such as education and career information, publications, continuing education classes, networking events, and mentoring programs. Many offer resources for middle and high school students, and some even allow them to become members. Let's take a look at some well-known engineering and science, technology, engineering, and math (STEM) associations to give you an idea of the resources that are available.

The Society of Manufacturing Engineers (SME) offers free membership for high school students. If you join the association, you'll receive *Manufacturing Engineering* magazine and access to the *SME Connect* blog, a mentorship program, scholarships, and competitions.

High school students who are considering a career in aerospace engineering can sign up for a free membership to the American Institute of Aeronautics and Astronautics. If you join the world's largest aerospace technical society, you'll receive access to a mentorship program, a daily newsletter, an online subscription to the magazine *Aerospace America*, and other resources. Student members can also compete in the organization's annual design challenges in a variety of aerospace technical fields. And anyone who visits the institute's website can download *Careers in Aerospace*, a short publication that offers advice on what students can do in high school to prepare for the field.

There are many other associations that provide resources for young people, many of which can be accessed online. For example, the American Society of Civil Engineers offers career articles and videos, competitions, lesson plans to try some civil engineering projects at home, and the opportunity to participate in an email or video chat with a civil engineer.

ASM International provides memberships for middle school and high school students and runs a material science camp for teens. The camp is held at ASM's headquarters in Novelty, Ohio. The National Society of Black Engineers offers membership for students in grades three through twelve, technical competitions, access to scholarships and awards, and mentorship or tutoring from college students or current STEM professionals. The Society of Women Engineers allows membership for young people between the ages of thirteen and eighteen, access to the organization's High School Leadership Academy and other events, competitions, and monthly newsletters that provide career advice and scholarship tips.

Attend a Camp

Tents, bug bites, and smoky campfires may come to mind when you hear the word *camp*. But don't despair if that's not your style. Engineering and other STEM camps are typically held in classrooms, laboratories, and workshops. You'll certainly spend some time outside conducting experiments and building drones, but you won't camp at the end of your day. Rather, you'll sleep in college dorms or, if you're attending a commuter camp, head home.

High schools, colleges and universities, professional associations, museums, and other organizations and groups offer camps. They are very popular for students to explore careers and have some fun. Each camp operates differently. They can last anywhere from one day to several weeks or more. Summer camps are the most popular options, but camps are also offered on weekends or during holiday breaks year-round. It's free to attend some camps, while others charge a program fee that typically ranges from one hundred dollars to thousands of dollars. But don't worry, many programs offer scholarships and other funding too. You may need to meet eligibility requirements such as a minimum age or minimum GPA to attend some camps. At some college- and university-sponsored programs, high school participants can even earn college credit.

Camps are available throughout the United States and in other countries. One popular camp is the Try Engineering Summer Institutes. The Institute of Electrical and Electronics Engineers sponsors them at different college campuses each year. Programs have been available at the University of Pennsylvania in Philadelphia, University of San Diego in San Diego, Columbia University in New York, and Rice University in Houston, Texas. Residential and commuter programs are available in civil, aerospace, electrical, mechanical, chemical, and computer engineering. Examples of past program activities include designing, 3D printing, assembling, and testing a light sculpture; constructing small bridges of increasing complexity of materials and durable strength; assembling and preparing a hydraulic robot arm; and building a fully operational AM radio from a kit. In addition to academic offerings, participants can attend movies, engage in karaoke competitions, try a climbing wall, and hang out with other campers. They also take field trips to job sites such as the Johnson Space Center and talk with engineers about their careers. A program fee is required, but scholarships are available. More information is available online.

Enter a Competition

Engineering and other STEM competitions allow you to

compete as an individual or as a member of a team against individuals or teams from other schools. Some competitions give winners certificates, but others may give out cash prizes, scholarships, trips to sponsor events, and other prizes. Regardless of whether you receive a prize, participation in competitions looks good on college applications. Competitions are also a way to develop engineering skills, build friendships, and have fun.

Professional associations, government science organizations, high schools, museums, and colleges and universities offer competitions for young people. One example is the Technology Student Association, which offers the Tests of Engineering Aptitude, Mathematics, and Science—an annual, themed competition for middle and high school students. In this one-day competition, teams of two to four students work together to complete an essay, answer multiple-choice questions, and finish a design/build challenge that's based on a theme that the National Academy of Engineering Grand Challenges highlights. Past themes include "Engineering and Everyday Devices" and "Engineering Another World." Teams first compete at the state level, and top scorers advance to the national competition. You do not need to be a member of the Technology Student Association to participate, but members receive a discount off the competition registration fee.

Join a Club

Most schools have engineering or general science clubs that you can join to get hands-on experience in your field of interest. Others may have aeronautic, makerspace robotics, 3D printing, and rocketry clubs. Depending on the club,

Building things can be fun and a great way to develop your problem-solving skills.

you might practice designing and building things. Some clubs focus on building battle bots to compete in robotics competitions or on learning how to use 3D modeling engineering and architecture computer software. Clubs may bring in engineers, technicians, or engineering professors to present about their work. Or students may get to tour engineering firms, manufacturing plants, and other places, such as water treatment plants or solar farms, where engineers work. If your school doesn't offer such a club, you can ask a school counselor or science teacher to help you start one.

Get Involved in Hands-On Activities

There are many ways to develop your skills at home too. One way is by building. You could build something electric such as an electrical circuit, a mini wind turbine or solar panel, a robot, or an electric- or solar-powered skateboard. Or you could build a structure such as an Archimedes screw (an ancient water pump), a marble roller coaster, a balloon-powered mini-car, or a mini-wind tunnel. You could even try building a home water filtration system. You can find instructions on how to build these and other things online and in books. But make sure to talk to or work with a trusted adult.

Participate in an Information Interview

During an information interview, you ask a professional questions about their background and job duties to obtain a better understanding of a particular career and how to prepare for it. You are not seeking a job at an information interview. Your number-one goal should be to obtain useful information. Your secondary goal should be to make networking contacts that might help lead to an internship or another exploration opportunity—or possibly even a job once you complete your training.

"These interviews can happen over coffee, at an office, on the phone, or virtually," according to the Columbia University Center for Career Education. "As you develop and strengthen your relationships over time, these relationships may help you discover unadvertised opportunities." Here are some questions to ask during an informational interview, though you can ask anything you are curious about:

- What made you want to enter this career?

- How did you prepare for this career?
- What's a typical day like on the job?
- Can you describe your work environment?
- Do you travel for your job? If so, to where and how often?
- What do you like most and least about your career?
- What types of equipment, tools, and software do you use to do your job? What are the most challenging ones to use?
- What are the key skills for people in your career? Have some skills become more important in recent years?
- What is the job outlook in your career? How will the field change in the next decade?
- What should I do now to prepare for the field?
- What professional or trade associations do people in your profession join?
- Are you certified? If so, what did you have to do to become certified, and how important is certification to career success?

You could ask your school counselor or science teacher to recommend someone you can interview. Perhaps your guardians or other family or household members can suggest some engineering professionals that you can interview. And some engineering associations have created programs that help students connect with members. For example, the American Society of Civil Engineers offers the Chat with a Civil Engineer program, which allows students to set up a video or email conversation with an engineer.

Participate in a Job Shadow

A job shadow experience involves observing a professional as they do their work. It can last anywhere from an hour to an entire workday and helps you see what a career is like and learn what you might like and dislike about it. As you job shadow someone in engineering, you might watch an aeronautical engineer as they build and test new aircraft prototypes in a wind tunnel, observe a civil engineer at a construction site, or watch a genetic engineer conduct research in a laboratory. Perhaps you'll even get the chance to look through a microscope.

How do you arrange a job shadow? You can contact employers directly regarding potential opportunities. Some have established formal programs. Professional engineering associations, your school's career counselor or a science teacher, and social media are other sources of potential leads.

Take Worksite Tours

Some companies, government agencies, and other employers of engineering professionals provide tours for students and others who are interested in the field or in seeing a structure that engineers have helped design and build. For example, if you're around the Chicago area and are interested in water engineering, you can tour seven water reclamation plants that the Metropolitan Water Reclamation District of Greater Chicago manages. The district also offers virtual tours of its facilities. The Mount Wilson Observatory in Los Angeles offers tours that educate visitors about the mechanical, optical, and electrical details of its 60-inch (152-cm) and 100-inch (254-cm) telescopes, which were the largest in the world when they opened in 1908 and 1917, respectively. The

Nine Tips for a Job Shadow

Once you've scheduled a job shadow, you'll need to prepare for it. The following tips will help you to make the most of your experience:

1. Prepare questions that you want to ask during the job shadow and bring something to take notes on.
2. If you're not sure what the dress code is, wear business casual clothing such as slacks and a polo shirt.
3. Try to arrive about ten minutes early to show your commitment to the experience.
4. Turn off your phone or put it on airplane mode before the experience begins so it doesn't cause any distractions.
5. Demonstrate good body language and be enthusiastic during the experience. Examples of good body language include sitting straight and not slouching, making consistent eye contact, and smiling when appropriate. Examples of enthusiasm include taking notes during the interview and stating your strong interest in the job (if that's the case) at the end of the interview.
6. Try not to interrupt the job shadow provider as they do their work.
7. Do not touch machinery, personal items in workspaces, and other objects without permission.
8. Thank the provider at the end of the experience and send a written thank-you note by mail or email within one day of the job shadow.
9. Try to stay in touch with the person you shadowed; they may be able to provide you with career advice in the future or steer you toward internships or part-time jobs.

Camps, classes, and science center demonstrations are good ways to learn more about current trends in the engineering field.

Aerospace Corporation in El Segundo, California, offers tours of its facilities that include robotic challenges, virtual reality demonstrations, and even the possibility of seeing a simulated rocket launch. NASA offers tours at many of its facilities, including the Johnson Space Center in Houston; the Jet Propulsion Laboratory in Pasadena, California; and the Kennedy Space Center on Merritt Island, Florida. Finally, if you want to become a solar engineer, the American Solar Energy Society offers a National Solar Tour event each year. In 2023 the society organized tours at more than two thousand solar sites in forty-nine states, the District of Columbia, and Puerto Rico. The tour also has a virtual component.

Additional Exploration Opportunities

There are many ways to learn about engineering from home, at school or work, or in your community. Here are some more ways to learn about engineering:

- Watch *Dream Big: Engineering Our World*, a short documentary about engineering marvels, and other films about engineering.
- Join the Technology Student Association, a nonprofit organization that offers opportunities to develop your leadership skills and help your community, college scholarships, and the chance to participate in more than seventy competitions.
- Talk to your school counselor about career opportunities.
- Ask your school or local librarian to suggest books about engineering.
- Take college-level engineering classes while you're in high school.
- Participate in various events during National Engineers Week in February, which is run by the National Society of Professional Engineers.
- Join your local Scouts and earn merit badges in engineering, drafting, composite materials, chemistry, electronics, inventing, robotics, and other areas.
- Observe engineering classes at a local community college or a four-year school.
- Attend open houses at engineering apprenticeship and college programs.
- Intern, volunteer, or work part-time at a government agency or company that employs engineers.

Visit Science Museums

Science museums are great places to learn about STEM fields and participate in hands-on science and engineering activities. Some museums offer volunteer opportunities and summer programs for students. At the Orlando Science Center in Florida, you can visit its Kinetic Zone: Science in Motion exhibit, where you can build and launch air rockets, use pipes to build a model of a roller coaster, and experiment with circuits. Other exhibits include the Hive: A Makerspace, Fusion: A STEAM (science, technology, engineering, arts, and mathematics) Gallery, and Tiny Green Home. The center offers competitions and summer programs for young people. Its Catalyst Youth Volunteer Program helps middle school and high school students to develop their leadership and teamwork skills, while providing services to museum visitors.

But you don't have to be in Florida to find a museum. Many states have dedicated science museums or centers that offer similar activities.

CHAPTER FOUR

Preparing for a Career in Engineering

Most people prepare for careers in engineering by earning two- or four-year degrees in engineering from a college or university. But some receive their training through apprenticeships (primarily technicians and technologists) or the armed forces (technicians and other engineering support workers). Each potential training path offers a unique road into engineering.

High School

Your high school education will help prepare you for postsecondary engineering training. If they're offered at your school, engineering classes will definitely help. But you should also take science courses such as physics, chemistry, and earth science and mathematics courses because these offerings provide the educational framework that all engineers need.

Many other classes can round out your education and will be useful in an engineering career. For example,

English, speech, and writing classes help you develop your oral communication skills and learn how to write concise and error-free reports, memos, and emails. A foreign language class could allow you to better communicate with colleagues and clients who speak that language. Computer science, including data analytics, classes help you learn how to collect, manage, and analyze information. Studying philosophy and social studies helps develop your critical thinking and analytical skills. And business management can help prepare you in case you want to pursue a management position or start your own consulting firm later on.

Don't forget to participate in engineering clubs, competitions, summer programs, or other exploration activities in high school. These also help build your engineering knowledge and obtain experience.

College and University Training

Many aspiring engineering professionals attend a college or university to prepare for their careers. What level of degree they receive often depends on their goals. Engineering technicians, technologists, and laboratory technicians often only need an associate degree in engineering technology or laboratory testing. Engineers need a bachelor's degree, but some may obtain a master's degree as well. College professors and engineering managers typically earn a bachelor's and a master's degree. Some professors earn a doctorate instead or in addition to their master's degree, as do research engineers, who are engineers who complete high-level research in their fields.

Some engineers receive a general engineering degree,

usually a bachelor's of science in engineering. Other engineers earn specialized degrees in industrial, civil, petroleum, mechanical, manufacturing and design, or other engineering fields. Some students also earn undergraduate or graduate certificates in an emerging technology such as machine learning, quantum computing, or advanced robotics; project management; or another applicable field to improve their skills. Engineers who want to become managers or start their own companies often earn their master's degree specifically in engineering management, science management, or business administration.

In addition to classroom instruction, engineering students practice their skills in laboratory sessions, such as using computer-aided design software or troubleshooting malfunctioning electronics. Depending on the school, students can also often use their school's facilities outside of class, which lets them practice their work, develop their skills, and learn new technology. For example, the College of Engineering at the University of Georgia has an open-access Design and Discovery Lab. "Resources in the lab include presentation tools, graphics workstations, a large collaborative space, vented soldering stations, and 3D printing and digitizing (2D and 3D) capabilities," says the university. "Presentation tools include wireless-enabled projection, a smart podium, and markerboards."

Many students participate in at least one internship at a company, government agency, or other employer of engineering professionals while earning their degree. This gives them hands-on experience in engineering, helps them learn how to do high-quality engineering work, and allows them to network with other professionals. If you complete an internship, be sure to work hard because many employers use their internship programs to identify future employees.

Apprenticeships

An apprenticeship is a structured training program that combines classroom instruction with supervised practical experience. Unlike a college education, which requires students to pay tuition and other fees, apprenticeship programs are free. Apprentices actually earn while they learn, and their salary increases as they obtain experience. Apprentices are also paired with a mentor to help them achieve career success. In an apprenticeship program that is affiliated with a community college, apprentices may even receive academic credit for completing courses. This comes in handy if they'd like to earn a college degree or certificate in addition to their apprenticeship training. Trade unions, community colleges, companies (such as Lockheed Martin, Rolls-Royce, Toyota, and Google), and government agencies all offer apprenticeships.

A Registered Apprenticeship Program is one that is industry-evaluated and approved and validated by the US Department of Labor or a state apprenticeship agency. At the federal level, these are available for aerospace engineers, mechanical engineering technologists and technicians, and robotics technicians.

The typical requirements for those applying to an apprenticeship program include being at least eighteen years old, having a high school education, and passing at least one year of high school algebra. Applicants must also undergo a drug test to ensure they are not using any illegal substances and pass an aptitude (ability) test.

Military Training

The US military and armed forces in other countries train and employ engineering professionals. The branches of the US military—air force, army (including via its well-known Army Corps of Engineers, which provides engineering services in both military and civilian sectors), coast guard, marines, navy, and space force—provide a variety of options for engineers, technicians, and related workers. Engineers typically enter military service after first earning a bachelor's degree. Some of the careers available in the military include aerospace engineer, civil engineer, electrical and electronics engineer, marine engineer, nuclear engineer, and industrial engineer.

You can train for many lower-level engineering positions within the military. For example, those who want to become flight engineering technicians first complete basic training, where they learn the basic rules of being a soldier, expected level of physical fitness, and how to use weapons and defend themselves. Aspiring technicians then receive specialized training via classroom instruction and on-the-job experience in aircraft inspection and flight operations. Other potential military career paths for aspiring engineering technicians include surveying, mapping, and drafting technicians; avionics technicians; space operations specialists; and precision instrument and equipment repairers.

In February 2023, 48,557 people worked in engineering, science, and technical positions in the US Army.

Pros and Cons of Different Engineering Training Paths

Each engineering training path has possible pros and cons. Let's take a look at each path.

College and University Training

Most engineering professionals, especially engineers, receive their training in college or university.

Pros

- A college education provides a direct path to employment.
- Students receive extensive training via programs that last two to six years.

Cons

- The cost of college (especially four-year and graduate schools) is often very high, and graduates may have a lot of student debt.
- Those who want to enter the workforce more quickly may not prefer having to go to school first.

Apprenticeship Training

Apprenticeship programs for engineers are not as popular

in the United States as they are in European countries. But many aspiring technicians in the US prepare for the field via apprenticeships.

Pros

- Apprenticeship programs do not charge tuition, so graduates will have no student debt.
- Apprentices are paid while they learn, and their salary increases as they gain experience.
- Apprentices obtain hands-on experience as they learn.
- In some instances, apprenticeship programs are shorter than college programs.

Cons

- Apprenticeship programs do not exist for every engineering specialty.
- Some employers may prefer to hire workers who have completed college training programs.

Military Training

Engineers typically have earned a bachelor's degree before entering the military as officers. Aspiring engineering technicians and related workers enter the military as enlisted personnel and receive training while serving their country.

Pros

- Military personnel receive a salary as they train for their careers.
- Serving in the armed forces may allow you to travel and see the world.
- Many companies view job applicants who served in the military as stronger candidates because of their perceived higher levels of discipline and work ethic.

Cons

- You will need to make a service commitment of two to four years.
- You will have to wear a uniform and do what the military tells you to do.
- You may be assigned to a war zone or be required to work in other dangerous environments.

CHAPTER FIVE

The Future of Engineering

There are many opportunities for engineering professionals. Several popular engineering fields are growing. And emerging technologies are likely to change and expand the industry too.

Employment Outlook

Overall employment for engineering and architecture workers is projected to grow faster than the average for all careers from 2022 to 2032, according to the US Department of Labor. Opportunities will be especially abundant in aerospace, agricultural, biomedical, chemical, electronics, environmental, hardware, industrial, materials, and mechanical engineering. Demand is growing for engineering professionals for a variety of reasons. For one, there is a shortage of skilled engineering professionals in many specialties. And there's a need to replace current workers who leave the field to retire or work in other fields. Technological advances, such as those in robotics, artificial intelligence, and

A person works on a computer circuit board. Technological advancements may make such objects smaller, faster, or smarter in the future.

quantum computing, are creating new types of engineering specialties and a need to use these technologies to create innovative products, structures, and systems, as well as to improve existing ones. Plus, global challenges such as climate change and pollution are increasing the need for engineering professionals that can work on those issues.

The four largest engineering fields are industrial, civil, electrical and electronics, and mechanical. Each field has its own outlook. Employment of industrial engineers is projected to increase 12 percent from 2022 to 2032. This is much faster than the average for all occupations, 4 percent. Job opportunities are plentiful for industrial engineers because companies and other employers are increasingly focusing on reducing internal costs, such as those for labor, raw materials, and shipping. Industrial engineers can provide expert advice on how to improve production processes, convert human-run factories to largely automated ones, and identify other actions that will save money. Demand is especially strong in the manufacturing sector.

The Department of Labor predicts that employment of civil engineers will grow 5 percent from 2022 to 2032—also faster than the average for all careers. Demand for civil engineers is increasing because the United States' bridges, roads, water systems, buildings, and other infrastructure need repair and improvement. The American Society of Civil Engineers publishes *Report Card for America's Infrastructure* every four years. It assigns letter grades based on the physical condition of each type of infrastructure and provides guidance on how they can be improved. Its 2021 report awarded an overall C– grade to American infrastructure. That means a lot must be done to improve our infrastructure, and civil engineers, technicians, and technologists will be at the forefront of this work. Demand will also be strong for civil engineers who work on renewable energy projects, such as the construction of wind farms and solar arrays, as people seek to reduce climate change and pollution. There is also a need for engineers who design smart-road technology that is being developed for use with semiautonomous and autonomous vehicles.

Job opportunities for electrical and electronics engineers are projected to also grow 5 percent from 2022 to 2032. Demand is increasing because engineers are needed to develop cutting-edge consumer electronics, semiconductors, solar arrays, and communications technologies. Employment opportunities are expected to be especially abundant in wind

Job opportunities will be strong for many engineering occupations because technological advancements continue to create demand for skilled workers.

electric power generation (where employment is expected to increase by 54.9 percent by 2032) and solar electric power generation (52.2 percent by 2032).

Employment of mechanical engineers is projected to increase 10 percent from 2022 to 2032. Mechanical engineers are in steady demand because they have the skills to work on a variety of projects and in a wide range of industries. Demand for mechanical engineers will be strongest in the fast-growing field of wind electric power generation, where the Department of Labor expects employment to increase by 67.3 percent by 2032. There will also be ample job opportunities for mechanical engineers who work in general robotics, manufacturing automation, and semiconductor and other electronic component manufacturing.

Employment Outlook for Engineering Technicians and Technologists

Not interested in being an engineer? Opportunities for technicians and technologists are also largely expected to grow between 2022 and 2032. Some examples:

- aerospace engineering and operations technologists and technicians: +8 percent
- civil engineering technologists and technicians: +1 percent
- electrical and electronic engineering technologists and technicians: +1 percent
- environmental engineering technologists and technicians: +1 percent
- industrial engineering technologists and technicians: +3 percent
- mechanical engineering technologists and technicians: +1 percent
- mechatronics technologists and technicians: –3 percent

Emerging Technologies

Emerging technologies continue to change the work of engineers. Some of the major technologies that you'll need to be aware of as an engineering professional include AI and virtual and augmented reality.

The global artificial intelligence market size was valued at $137.67 billion in 2023, according to the market research company Research and Markets. Its value is projected to

Technicians are responsible for repairing and maintaining equipment to make sure it is fully operational.

reach nearly $1.06 trillion by 2030. Research and Markets says that "the reported growth stems from AI's capabilities in enhancing efficiencies, decision-making processes, and productivity across prominent industries—health care, finance, cybersecurity, and beyond. A surge in autonomous AI systems, capable of functioning independently, is particularly noted for its positive impact on the market's acceleration." Engineers will likely use AI and generative AI to collect and analyze information more quickly; write reports; improve productivity, safety, and the quality of products; complete design tasks; and meet other goals.

This technology can also be added to software, robots, manufacturing systems, and other structures and systems to save time and money, increase efficiency, and create new uses of existing products.

Engineers are using unmanned aerial vehicles—drones—to obtain images and video, as well as sensor readings, of hard to reach areas at construction sites, disaster sites, oil spills, and other places. This helps keep engineers safe.

Virtual and augmented reality are becoming popular tools for engineering professionals too. Engineers can use virtual reality technologies that are paired with building or other modeling software to walk around a virtual construction site to plan a project or show clients what a potential structure or product will look like before its creation.

Engineers can use augmented reality technology to collaborate with team members in different locations, to train workers, and for quality control purposes (that is, to identify human error in real time by virtually overlaying specifications and assembly instructions on a product or equipment that is being inspected). Engineers and technicians also use augmented reality glasses to visualize assembly instructions, which can either replace or add to complex written instructions. Engineering professionals can even use augmented reality technology to display designs in real time in a construction workspace or other setting to help them better understand how the design will look and function in the real world. And they can display conceptual designs on a computer as they are intended to look in the real world.

CONCLUSION

Putting It All Together

Becoming an engineer might be right for you if you enjoy designing and building structures, objects, and systems. Plus, many different career paths are available, job growth is strong, salaries are higher than the average, and no day is the same in this fast-changing field. Maybe you'll help design amusement park rides. Or you could help fix bridges in your city or develop a new system for creating or collecting renewable energy. No matter what field you pick, all engineering jobs come with the chance to complete hands-on work and even try out emerging technologies.

Now that you've read this book, you can continue exploring the field by participating in information interviews, attending summer camps, building things at home, and more. So get to work, have some fun in the process, and good luck with your career exploration.

GLOSSARY

3D printing: also called additive manufacturing, a manufacturing process in which a 3D object is created by adding successive layers of material

aerodynamics: the study of gases in motion

architecture: the process of using creativity and technical knowledge to design and build structures

artificial intelligence (AI): a form of computer science in which human intelligence is simulated by computer systems

augmented reality: a computer-generated system that combines a virtual environment that contains imaginary digital elements with the real world

circuit: two electrical devices that are connected and which transmit electricity to provide power to appliances, machinery, and other things

computer-aided design: the use of software to create blueprints, architectural plans, or artwork

computer modeling: the use of computers and the disciplines of mathematics, physics, and computer science to simulate and study complex systems and determine possible outcomes

design thinking: the process of solving complex problems by using a human-focused approach and outside-the-box thinking

energy: thermal (heat), electrical, chemical, light (radiant), kinetic (motion), nuclear, or gravitational energy that is harnessed to perform the functions of life

engineering design process: a series of steps that engineering professionals follow to solve problems. The steps are: identify the problem, conduct research, brainstorm and create a potential solution, develop a prototype solution, test solution, and communicate results.

generative AI: the use of machine learning algorithms to create new content including text, videos, simulations, images, audio, and computer code, as well as evaluate and organize vast amounts of data and other information

genome: the entire set of DNA instructions found in a cell

green construction: the use of building processes and eco-friendly building materials to create healthier buildings for their occupants and reduce the negative effects of their construction and operation on the environment

Internet of Things: a network of devices that contains sensors and other information-collecting technology, which connect to the cloud, as well as between themselves. Internet of Things applications are used in smart buildings, advanced manufacturing, connected cars, and smart buildings, among other areas.

makerspace: an area where students can use tools, materials, and machinery (such as 3D printers) to make things

nanotechnology: the manipulation of matter on a near-atomic scale to create new materials, structures, and devices

prototype: a working model of a product or information system that is created before the finished product or system is built

quantum computing: a field that uses specialized technology (including computer hardware and algorithms that take advantage of quantum mechanics) to solve complex problems that can't be solved as fast or at all by using classical computers or supercomputers

robotics: an area of computer science, artificial intelligence, and electronic, mechanical, and other types of engineering that involves the design, construction, testing, and operation of robots that perform tasks more efficiently and less expensively than can be done by humans

schematic diagram: an illustration that uses standardized symbols and simple line drawings to represent the components of a process, device, or other object

thermodynamics: the study of heat and other forms of energy

virtual reality: a computer-generated experience that takes place within a simulated environment, with users typically wearing a head-mounted display device or other wearable equipment to access the technology

SOURCE NOTES

6 "The engineer has . . . maker of history.": James Kip Finch, *The Story of Engineering* (Garden City, NY: Doubleday, 1960), xxvii.

14 "Nanotechnology is helping . . . among many others,": Applications of Nanotechnology, National Nanotechnology Initiative, accessed July 25, 2024, https://www.nano.gov/about-nanotechnology/applications-nanotechnology.

17 "When it comes . . . the project lifecycle.": "The Role of Engineering Technicians in Quality Control," MoldStud, January 16, 2024, https://moldstud.com/articles/p-the-role-of-engineering-technicians-in-quality-control.

36 "These interviews can . . . discover unadvertised opportunities.": "Informational Interviewing is Key to Your Job Search," Columbia University Center for Career Education, accessed July 25, 2024, https://www.careereducation.columbia.edu/resources/informational-interviewing-key-your-job-search.

46 "Resources in the . . . podium, and markerboards.": "Fabrication Labs," University of Georgia College of Engineering, accessed July 25, 2024, https://engineering.uga.edu/students/undergraduate/fabrication-labs/.

57 "the reported growth . . . the market's acceleration.": "Artificial Intelligence Market, Size, Global Forecast 2024–2030, Industry Trends, Share, Growth, Insight, Impact of Inflation, Company Analysis," Research and Markets, accessed July 25, 2024, https://www.researchandmarkets.com/report/artificial-intelligence.

SELECTED BIBLIOGRAPHY

"What Is Quantum Computing?" IBM. Accessed July 1, 2024. https://www.ibm.com/topics/quantum-computing.https://www.mtu.edu/engineering/outreach/welcome/engineers.

"What Is an Engineer?" Michigan Tech College of Engineering. Accessed July 1, 2024. https://www.mtu.edu/engineering/outreach/welcome/engineers.

"Key Skills Employers Seek in Engineers." Engineering and Technology Jobs, November 17, 2023. https://engineering-jobs.theiet.org/article/key-skills-employers-seek-in-engineers.

"Architecture and Engineering Occupations." Occupational Outlook Handbook. Accessed July 1, 2024. https://www.bls.gov/ooh/architecture-and-engineering.

"Science, Technology, Engineering, and Mathematics." Today's Military. Accessed July 1, 2024. https://www.todaysmilitary.com/careers-benefits/career-fields/science-technology-engineering-mathematics.

FURTHER INFORMATION

Books

Estes, Fred. *Design Thinking: A Guide to Innovation.* Minneapolis: Zest Books, 2025.
This book provides an overview of how design thinking is used to solve human-centered, social issues. It features stories of how student teams are using design thinking to change and improve the world.

Estes, Fred. *Teen Innovators: Nine Young People Engineering a Better World with Creative Inventions.* Minneapolis: Zest Books, 2022.
This book tells the stories of young people who used their creativity and engineering knowledge to improve the world. Examples include designing and building a device to detect lead in drinking water, creating an improvised electrical generator using a windmill, and creating a digital display glove to aid people who have a speech impairment.

Hillhouse, Grady. *Engineering in Plain Sight: An Illustrated Field Guide to the Constructed Environment.* San Francisco: No Starch Press, 2022.
A civil engineer and science communicator explains how engineering principles are used to design and build roads, railways, bridges, electrical grid, tunnels, waterways, and other types of infrastructure.

McCauley, Pamela. *Engineering for Teens: A Beginner's Book for Aspiring Engineers.* Emeryville, CA: Rockridge Press, 2021.
In this book, you'll learn about the four main branches of engineering and their different specialties, the history of the field, famous engineers in history, and women in engineering.

Smil, Vaclav. *Invention and Innovation: A Brief History of Hype and Failure.* Cambridge, MA: MIT Press, 2023.
It's easy to take engineering achievements for granted, but a lot of trial and error goes into inventing new things and improving existing products and systems. Smil takes a deep dive into the history of human invention. He spotlights both successful inventions and those that were harmful rather than helpful.

Websites

Discover Engineering

https://discovere.org/stem-careers

Check out detailed information about fifteen engineering specialties and ten reasons why engineering is a popular career field and read short interviews with engineers.

EngineerGirl

www.engineergirl.org

This website is a service of the National Academy of Engineering. It features interviews with women engineers and information on engineering careers, clubs, competitions, and scholarships. You can also learn more about trailblazing women engineers.

Explore Engineering

https://exploreengineering.ca

This website from Engineers Canada offers an overview of the different engineering specialties, interviews with engineers about their backgrounds and careers, information on educational requirements, exploration activities including quizzes to test your engineering knowledge, and other resources.

How to Get Started

www.nacme.org/engage-highschool#becomeAnEngineer

The National Action Council for Minorities in Engineering provides information on engineering specialties, how you can prepare for the field, and what you can do to learn more about engineering. The council also offers the *NACME Guide to Engineering Colleges*.

TryEngineering

https://tryengineering.org/students

This website offers information on more than twenty engineering, technology, and computer fields. It also provides profiles of engineers; an Ask an Expert section, in which engineers respond to common questions about education and careers; information on exploration opportunities such as camps; and games, which students can play to have fun and increase their engineering knowledge.

INDEX

ABOUT THE AUTHOR

Andrew Morkes is the founder and editorial director of College & Career Press in Chicago, Illinois. He has written about college- and career-related topics for more than thirty years. Morkes is the author of more than sixty books about college planning and careers, including many titles in the Vault Career Guides series (including *Cybersecurity, Law, Pharmaceuticals and Biotechnology, and Information Technology),* and *They Teach That in College!?: A Resource Guide to More Than 100 Interesting College Majors,* which was selected as one of the best books of the year by the library journal *Voice of Youth Advocates*. He is also the author and publisher of *The Morkes Report: College and Career Planning Trends* blog. Morkes is a member of the parent advisory board at his son's school. He is also the author of *Nature in Chicagoland: More Than 120 Fantastic Nature Destinations That You Must Visit.* Articles about Morkes's work have appeared in the *Chicago Tribune, Chicago Sun-Times, Practical Homeschooling*, and other publications.

PHOTO ACKNOWLEDGMENTS

Image credits: EAKARAT BUANOI/Shutterstock, p.5; Brownie Harris/ The Image Bank/Getty Images, p.9; Monstar Studio/Shutterstock, p.13; sinology/Moment/Getty Images, p.16; Jacques Tarnero/Shutterstock, p. 25; xavierarnau/E+/Getty Images, p.26; BAZA Production/ Shutterstock, p.33; svetikd/E+/Getty Images, p.38; M_Agency/ Shutterstock, p.46; enigma_images/E+/Getty Images, p. 49; Catchawal Phumkaew/Shutterstock, p.51; Gorondenkoff/Shutterstock, p. 53

Cover image: Westend61/Getty Images